Privacy

Deal with it

like nobody's business

Diane Peters • Illustrated by Jeremy Tankard

James Lorimer & Company Ltd., Publishers
Toronto

You just spent the night at a friend's.

You get home, and your room doesn't seem right.

You look around and realize that someone — probably your little brother — has looked through your desk, your closet, and even your dresser drawers! You're so upset you could scream. **Your privacy has just been invaded.**

Everybody has thoughts and possessions and secrets they don't want other people to hear or see. When someone's private things are revealed to others without their permission, that's an invasion of privacy.

Sometimes invasions of privacy, or intrusions, are not done on purpose. The intruder may not know something was private or that digging around would hurt anyone.

Maybe you're wondering if you have ever crossed the line.

It can sometimes be hard to know the difference between just being interested or concerned and intruding on someone else's privacy.

Intentional or not, privacy intrusions can lead to hurt feelings, misunderstandings, embarrassment, and conflict with others.

In this book, you'll learn more about privacy — what it is, what can happen when it's invaded, and what you can do to cope when conflicts arise.

Contents

What is

So, you know what to keep under wraps, don't you?

We all have things that we want to keep to ourselves or to share with only close friends or family. Some things you probably want to keep private are:

- your diary

- your feelings about someone

- your bedroom

- a box of keepsakes

- a letter from someone close to you

- personal e-mails

- certain parts of your body

- your family's financial information, like how much money your parents earn.

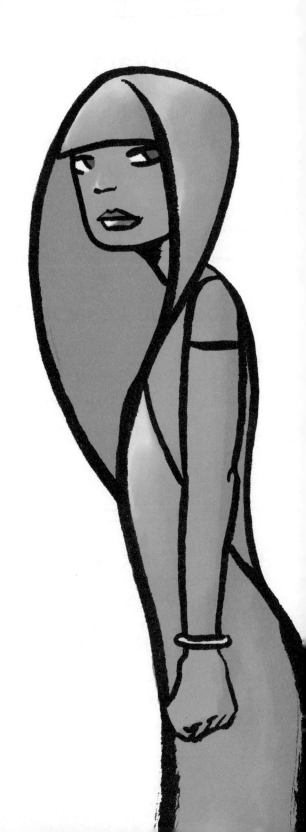

Privacy?

But what's private can be different for different people. And something that is normally out in the open might need to be private in certain situations. What about:

- creative things like a song, drawing, or poem?

- where you live or your phone number?

- details about your health?

- a phone conversation?

- your age?

- other parts of the body, like the arms or head?

- your identity in an anonymous situation?

- how much allowance you receive or how much you get paid for something?

Are these things private? They can be, since revealing them could cause people embarrassment or even harm.

Privacy 101

Privacy helps people *protect*

This is kind of secret but... Alicia's dad got arrested!

I can't believe it!

How awful!

I knew he was bad news!

Maybe I shouldn't have said that...

BRIT SITS AT RASHAD'S COMPUTER AND READS THE SCREEN.

Rashad, your answers were suspiciously similar to Brit's.

?

You can see right into Cera's window from here. She's taking her clothes off!

I don't want to tell on Ethan...

...but poor Cera!

LATER THAT NIGHT...

CALDER WALKS IN TO FACE AN ANGRY OLDER BROTHER.

I can't believe what I heard today!

Oh NO!

7

QUIZ

What do you call nobody's business?

What should be kept private depends on the person and the situation. Take this quiz to see if you can tell when privacy is at stake. Decide if each of the following is an invasion of privacy or not. Check your answers on the next page.

1 **Dress Code**
Anya's mother always walks into her room without knocking — even when Anya is in the middle of changing! In fact, they often start talking about what Anya's planning to wear that day.

2 **Unlisted**
Joe has the unlisted phone number of his friend Robbie. When a girl Robbie likes asks for it, Joe gives her the number.

3 **Share the Music**
Bill loves writing songs, and often plays them for his family. One day, his brother takes one of the lyric sheets to school and shows his friends.

4 **Medical Mystery**
Annabelle is having surgery to have a lump removed from an embarrassing place. All week, while she's off, her close friends explain her absence with, "It's a secret." By the time Annabelle returns to school, there are dozens of rumours about her.

5 **Private Poet**
For his final English project, Jordan hands in a book of very personal poems he has written. When the teacher is handing the projects back, she accidentally gives Jordan's to someone else. A few kids in class end up reading his poems.

6 Swimming the Web
Somehow, pictures of Allison in her swimsuit get posted on the Internet. Allison thinks she looks good in the pictures. She even e-mailed them to a bunch of people, which might be how they got on the Net.

7 The Crush
Brendan is madly in love with Eva. He has told every guy in class and, eventually, someone tells Eva.

8 Blabbing about Bedwetting
Eleanor is having great fun swapping stories with her friends. She tells them that her sister was wetting the bed until only recently. That gets a lot of laughs. But the next day, the story starts spreading around school.

9 Keeping a Low Profile
Ali's family came to Canada to escape war. The family changed their last name when they emigrated, and keep a low profile. Ali tells this to his class in a presentation. His parents get upset, even though nothing happens as a result.

10 Private Period
Mona is in a crabby mood. Her friend Elizabeth says, "Mona, you are PMSing so bad. Take a Midol or go home already." Mona laughs, but some of the girls in the group are totally shocked.

Answers

1. No. Anya doesn't consider her room or her body private from her mother.

2. Yes. The privacy of Joe's whole family has been put at risk. Joe could have arranged for Robbie to call this girl instead.

3. Yes. Just because Bill doesn't keep his songs private from his family doesn't mean he wants to share them with everyone.

4. No. Annabelle's friends do keep the secret, but they could have offered a less suspicious sounding explanation.

5. Yes. Even though it was an accident, the teacher owes Jordan an apology.

6. No. Allison clearly doesn't consider these pictures private. For another person, however, this could be a very traumatic invasion of privacy.

7. No. Brendan didn't tell Eva directly about his feelings, but he made no attempt to keep them private.

8. Yes. Eleanor told this embarrassing story and invaded her sister's privacy just to entertain her friends.

9. Yes. Since it was the family's wish that this be kept private, and since it's hard to know in advance what the consequences of a told secret can be, Ali should not have shared this information with the whole class.

10. No. Elizabeth seems to understand that her friend won't feel embarrassed about the teasing. Others might feel differently in this situation.

Dear Privacy Counsellor

Q. My brother and I share a room. He's totally insane about "his side." If I even put a shoe over there, he gets really upset. He acts like every time I walk into the room, I'm invading his privacy. But it's my room too!

— *Sharing with Mr. Private*

A. It's hard to be sympathetic about how someone else feels when you don't feel the same way. But if your brother has strong feelings about privacy in your shared room, you should try to respect that. Try talking to him about why you feel differently about the room. See if it would help if you knocked before coming in when you know he is there, and try to stay away from his "side" and his stuff. If he knows that you are not crowding him on purpose, and you are trying to respect his feelings, he may not feel like his privacy is being threatened all the time.

Q. My best friend just told me that she saw her stepfather hit her mother. She begged me not to tell anyone. I don't know what to do! I'm really scared for both her and her mom. Will I invade her privacy by telling? — *Got an Awful Secret*

A. There are times when it's not a good idea to keep a secret. Right now, you might want to continue talking to your friend and help her find a way to share her problems with someone who can help. But if you think your friend is being hurt, you must report it. If nothing changes, you might want to talk to your parents about what to do. Just be sure to tell your friend when you do, and don't spread word around school that this is going on.

Q. I just made a new friend and she's not private about anything at all! I already know everything about her family, including how much money they make. When I go to her place, everyone is talking about who they like and who they've kissed in front of everyone — parents included! Sometimes, I feel a little overwhelmed around her and her family. I'm so used to keeping this stuff to myself at home. —*T(oo) M(uch) I(nformation)*

A. Every family defines privacy differently, and it sounds like your friend and her family have boundaries that are way out there! Try to respect their ways when you're there and avoid judging them. That said, you don't have to suddenly change your ways to fit in. When issues of your own privacy come up, make sure your friend respects your boundaries. If she just doesn't get it, remember that you don't have to be friends with everyone, and you have every right to end friendships that make you uncomfortable.

Q. My mother is a police officer. My parents refuse to give out our phone number and don't even want me telling anyone but close friends where we live! My new friends don't understand this at all, and I kind of agree with them that my family is being paranoid. — *Nameless*

A. It sounds like your parents are worried that your family will be harassed or put in danger because of your mother's job. Try to respect their wishes. Your mother, or her co-workers, may have had bad experiences in the past that have taught them to be extra careful. Explain to your friends the reason why your family guards your privacy and they might understand better too.

Myths

There's no such thing as privacy inside a FAMILY.

Even people who live in the same house have a right to their private things, thoughts, and actions being left alone.

Things that are just lying around are no longer private.

The most private of things can be left out in plain sight by accident, or by someone invading a person's privacy.

If someone is KEEPING a secret for the wrong reasons, it's okay to tell it.

Unless the secret is putting that person in danger, it's still a privacy invasion to tell others. In most cases, what should be kept private is up to the person concerned.

DID YOU KNOW ?

- In 2003, Canadians lost $21 million because of identity theft. This is when someone uses your name and personal

If I **don't need** to keep it **private**, the same goes for **everyone else**.

Different people consider different things private. It's important to respect others and not assume they feel the same as you.

If you're **not told** something is a secret **it's okay** to tell it.

Usually, you know if something's a secret or not without being told. (If you're not sure, ask!) Sharing something private can hurt feelings or cause problems whether you've "zipped your lips" or not.

If it won't **hurt** someone to tell a secret, it's **okay** to tell.

When you're asked to keep a secret, it's best to do so. You don't really know if someone will get hurt, or who it might be. We can't foresee all the consequences of our actions, so keeping a secret is usually the right way to go.

info so they can steal or borrow money under your name.	• Canada, like other nations, has laws that dictate how personal	information about you can be used.	• By law, if you know of a child at risk or being hurt, you must report it.

Your secret is out!

It's all around your friends and family, the neighbourhood, your school.

How did this happen? How did everyone find out about your private life? Now you probably feel:

- embarrassed
- betrayed
- angry
- hurt
- revengeful
- afraid for your safety
- depressed
- ashamed
- or exposed.

These feelings can lead to conflict between you and the person who invaded your privacy, or with others who now know your darkest secrets.

DEAR DR. SHRINK-WRAPPED . . .

Q. I write all my personal thoughts in my journal. The other day, I found my mother reading it. I got really mad, but she said "I'm your mother, you shouldn't be keeping anything from me." Is she right?

— *Dear Diary*

A. There's no right or wrong when it comes to personal privacy, Dear. Your privacy is how you define it, not what someone else thinks. While Dr. Shrink-Wrapped doesn't like to say that anyone's mother is wrong, I think you do have a right to privacy, even within your family. If that's not your family's tradition, it may be more difficult for you to convince your mother of this.

I suggest you keep your journal well hidden and try to explain that, while she is your mother and you love her, you are also an individual person who is entitled to your own privacy rights.

Q. My best friend is from a different cultural background than I am. She says that in her culture they talk about money all the time, but my family doesn't. She gets offended when I don't want to tell her what my parents make or how much money we spent on certain things. I know I'm hurting her feelings. What should I do?   — *Friendly Finances*

A. Dr. Shrink-Wrapped knows that cultural differences are tough. We learn many values from our family background, and it's hard sometimes to learn about or accept other values. But, Friendly, if you don't want to talk about money with your friend, you don't have to. To help her understand, try talking calmly about the issue. Tell her it's not something you're doing to hurt her feelings, but you're simply not comfortable talking about money.

Want to make sure your private stuff stays under wraps? There are some simple things you can do to protect your privacy.

Help others help you
When you tell a secret, make sure you make it clear that the information is private. If people need to provide an explanation to protect your privacy, give them suggestions. "If someone asks where I was, tell them…"

Set boundaries
Make it clear — even to your close friends and family members — what you consider private.

Choose your confidantes wisely
Don't tell a secret to someone you know might tell it, or to someone you know will be pressured to tell by others.

Protect your stuff
Keep your private writing, letters, and journals safe by leaving them at home. In your backpack, your locker, or the family car they're always at risk of being seen or lost.

DID YOU KNOW?

- People can use certain personal information to commit crimes.

Always make sure you keep these things private from strangers:

do's and don'ts

✓ Do believe you have a right to keep things private.

✓ Do define privacy for yourself.

✓ Do protect your personal belongings and information.

✓ Do find a loyal friend who can keep a secret to share private things with.

✓ Do learn about your privacy rights.

✓ Do report privacy violations to an adult.

✓ Do continue to be creative.

✓ Do tell others how you feel about privacy, whether they're family members or friends.

Respect others
Listen to what others say about their own privacy. They'll do the same for you in return.

Ask for help
Turn to a trustworthy adult if you're having problems keeping something private.

✗ Don't let others tell you what is private and what is not.

✗ Don't bring private things to school or other places that put them at risk.

✗ Don't keep secrets or hold on to private information that could put you or others in danger.

✗ Don't let shame prevent you from doing the things you want.

✗ Don't invade others' privacy as retaliation.

- your name and social insurance number
- your address
- the fact you spend time alone at home or work
- your phone number
- the type of car your family drives
- details about your home, such as a broken lock or window.

When the Media is Involved

Privacy is a word you hear a lot these days. It's a complicated world, and keeping things private isn't just about keeping someone from reading your diary or having a secret crush on someone. When can keeping something private — or invading someone's privacy — be a crime?

Personal Information

Canada has special laws to protect people's private information. These laws control how institutions like government agencies, doctors' offices, and banks deal with this information. These types of institutions need the information to help people, but in the wrong hands it could lead to people being victims of discrimination and crime.

Personal information includes:

*   address and phone number
*   how much money someone makes and has saved
*   medical history
*   credit rating (a rating that says how reliable someone is at paying off debts)
*   history of marriages and divorces

Online Security

Where is personal information most at risk? You got it: online. Web sites that collect information from you — like asking for your home and e-mail address before letting you use a free service like a game or a newsletter — can give it away or sell it to others. This might result in you getting junk e-mail and junk mail, which is annoying. But it can also lead to identity theft, which is a serious crime.

*   It is legal to tape conversations (such as over the phone) if you are one of the people talking. However, you cannot tape two

Another time to think about your privacy online is when you buy something. You might not think twice about giving a credit card number to get those cool sneaks or a new DVD, but some Web sites are not honest. When you buy something with a credit card number, it can lead to someone else using that number to buy things. Whenever you're online, it's very important to control how much information you give out. Make sure the Web site you're visiting is legitimate, and watch for messages about security measures they have in place to protect your information. If the Web site has a recognizable name and people you know have used it safely, it should be okay.

Safety vs. Personal Freedom

Countries and businesses want to keep people safe from terrorists and criminals. You've probably seen video cameras at bank machines, at airports, in elevators, and even in the street. Some places use technology to read your fingerprints or the retina of your eye before you're let in a door. And some countries make people show ID cards when they travel.

Many people are concerned that these types of safety devices, while protecting us, also limit our freedom and privacy. The technology allows others to see us in moments that we thought were private, and might even limit the places we go. How much information about us do the government and businesses need? How much is too much? When does protecting us end and invading our lives begin? Only you can answer these questions about you.

other people talking without their permission.

- Personal information (phone numbers and addresses) of people like judges, lawyers, and police officers are often kept secret. This keeps these individuals and their families safe.

What's the big deal?

You're just sort of a nosy person. You sometimes look into places you shouldn't. You sometimes try to find information about people. But you're not breaking any laws. You're not causing harm — **are you?**

Hurting Others

There's no way you can foresee what the result of your snooping might be. There might be reasons that people want to keep things private that you have no clue about — until it's too late. How would you feel if your curiosity led to someone being embarrassed, discriminated against, afraid for their safety, or even arrested or hurt?

Hurting Yourself

If you're known as a privacy invader, people may have a hard time trusting you. When even your closest friends don't share their secrets with you, and when family members feel they have to keep their stuff hidden or under lock and key, you'll probably start feeling cut off from the people you care about. It hurts when people don't trust you, and it's always way harder to win back that trust than to lose it in the first place.

do's and don'ts

✓ Do respect others' wishes with regard to their privacy.

✓ Do discuss privacy issues with friends and family.

✓ Do define how you feel about your own private things and ideas.

✗ Don't pass on rumours about someone's private life or feelings.

✗ Don't try to break locks/descramble passwords to get to something.

✓ Do keep a secret when you're told one.

✓ Do remember how good it feels when people trust you.

✓ Do avoid getting sucked into gossip.

✓ Do ask people what they consider private.

✓ Do stop and think before you act or speak.

✓ Do feel satisfied not knowing everything.

✓ Do understand that there are many reasons why someone might keep something private that has nothing to do with your trustworthiness.

✓ Do let someone know if it will be difficult for you to keep a secret *before* they tell you.

✗ Don't consider it your right to know everything about everyone.

✗ Don't pressure others to reveal secrets.

✗ Don't promise to keep a secret if you think you'll be tempted to share it.

✗ Don't drop hints about private information if you're not supposed to reveal it.

QUIZ

Curious cat or privacy invader?

Do you love knowing dirty little secrets and digging into private things? Take this quiz to find out more about yourself. Of the following statements, which ones are true about you and which ones false?

1 I love reading gossip in newspapers and magazines.

2 When things about others don't make total sense, I have to know the reasons why.

3 I love talking about other people.

4 I'm really curious about everything.

5 I have a hard time understanding why people don't feel the same way I do.

6 I love reading people's letters and writing.

7 If I don't think telling a secret will hurt anyone, I'll tell it.

8 When people say, "Don't tell anyone," I don't always believe they mean it.

9 I like to know a lot about people — about their families and their feelings and stuff.

10 Telling a secret or gossiping in person is the same as writing it down or putting it on the Internet.

I think if I know more about someone, I could help them. **11**

People are too touchy about privacy. **12**

I don't believe people should keep secrets. **13**

I like to know what people do in their private lives. **14**

I get bored with the usual gossip: I like to find out the really juicy stuff. **15**

I have a hard time knowing when something should be kept private or not. **16**

I find it really funny when certain private things get told in public. You get the best laughs from these things. **17**

I've had people not tell me stuff. They tell me, "You can't keep a secret." **18**

If someone wants to spread gossip, they come to me. **19**

I've had some conflicts with people in the past over told secrets or exposed private stuff. **20**

Did you score a lot of trues? You might have an issue with not respecting other people's privacy. Maybe it's time to talk to someone about becoming more trustworthy.

The **Intruder**

How to Respect Privacy

Are people afraid to leave you alone with their private stuff? Do people make sure to keep their deepest secrets from you? Here are some ways you can help yourself and others learn to respect privacy.

Listen to others. Some people like to read their love letters aloud while others hate people even stepping in their bedroom door. Listen to your friends to find out how they define privacy for themselves.

Ask questions. If someone tells you something, ask if it's a secret or not. Find out who you can and cannot tell.

Stop and think. Before you pick up that diary or open your mouth to share a secret, think first. Ask yourself the following:

*   could this be a private thing I'm about to invade?

*   would doing this hurt someone else's feelings if they found out?

*   would I want someone to do this to me?

*   am I being nosy, or do I have a good reason for doing this?

Think about it. Reconsider your definition of privacy for yourself. There's nothing wrong with

DID YOU KNOW?

*   The phrase "Big Brother is watching" is from a book titled *1984* by George Orwell. The book is about a very rigid society where citizens have no freedom and

DEAR DR. SHRINK-WRAPPED . . .

Q. My friend's dad lost his job, and he wanted me to keep it a secret. I didn't think it was such a big deal because I know lots of people who have lost their jobs. Anyway, I told my girlfriend — she's cool, and I would tell her absolutely anything about my own life. My friend found out and he's so mad he won't be my friend anymore. Isn't he overreacting?

— *Lost Job Equals Lost Friend*

A. Hey, Lost, the thing about privacy is that it's a very personal thing. While you might not think someone losing a job is a big deal, your friend obviously did. And whether or not you feel it is about anything important, it is important to keep secrets. That's how Dr. Shrink-Wrapped shows respect for people and acts like a good friend.

The other thing you have to realize is that, when you reveal a secret, there can be consequences you might not have thought of. Some consequences might be:

- feelings of shame for your friend with the secret
- your friend having to deal with the direct consequences of the secret
- others treating your friend differently
- legal problems if a law has been broken
- problems for family members, other friends, or people indirectly involved in the secret
- loss of trust, or even a friendship.

---

changing your boundaries and expecting others to respect that.

Avoid gossip. A lot of the time, gossip about people involves revealed secrets. Refuse to pass on gossip that you hear.

Question your own nosiness. Look into your own motivations for wanting to know private things about others. Consider taking on a new hobby to keep yourself interested in your own life.

---

are being watched all the time.

- Mail coming into Canada that weighs less than 30 grams cannot be opened without consent. However, packages over 30 grams that seem suspicious can be opened by a Canada Customs officer.

The **Witness**

You can't believe your eyes. You've just seen someone pick up a top-secret piece of paper, read it, and then share it with the rest of the room.

How could someone be so insensitive? But the next question is the big one:

What to do next?

Witnesses have choices

Here are some ways you could respond to seeing a privacy invasion:

- tell the invader what you saw and what you think of their actions
- find the person whose privacy has been invaded and tell them about it
- turn away from the situation.

You might respond in any of these ways, depending on the situation. But consider putting yourself in the place of the person whose privacy has been invaded. What kind of response would you want from someone?

Witnesses have the power

Although you might be good at minding your own business, being a witness to an invasion of privacy might call on you to get involved.

People who invade the privacy of others usually care a lot about what people are thinking and saying about people, especially about themselves. Calling a privacy invader on intrusive behaviour shows that the gossip can just as easily turn on the one telling the secret or exposing the information.

Remember, you have the power to make the situation worse or better.

do's and don'ts

✓ Do stop and consider all your options before reacting.

✓ Do remember that your response could influence the people involved.

✓ Do take measures to ensure your privacy and others'.

✓ Do talk about respecting others' privacy.

✓ Do refuse to spread secrets or rumours.

✓ Do inform the exposed person about what is going on.

✓ Do tell people exposed by an invasion of privacy that you support them.

✓ Do report the incident if it's serious or someone is in danger.

✓ Do confide in a close friend or adult.

✗ Don't get sucked into invading privacy too.

✗ Don't encourage an invader.

✗ Don't ignore unacceptable behaviour.

✗ Don't laugh at or shame a person who has been exposed.

✗ Don't help justify an invasion by saying things like "It's no big deal."

QUIZ

① SECRET NUMBER

Everyone in the family knows your mother is very sensitive about her age. At a family reunion, you hear your sister telling a crowd about your mom's birthday the following week and just how old she'll be. What should you do?

- Pull your sister aside and ask her to respect your mother's privacy, whether or not she agrees that age is a big deal.
- Warn your mother that someone is telling others about her age.
- You might not want to name names here, since telling tales puts you in a bad position and might get your sister punished.

Do you really get it?

You understand the value of privacy, but do you know what you'd do if you saw it being invaded? Read the following situations and think about what you'd do. This quiz has no right or wrong answers, because each situation is unique. Your answers may be different from the ones given, but they could be right under the circumstance.

② STUCK IN THE MIDDLE

Your dad is convinced your big brother is doing drugs. He has started snooping in your brother's room, hoping to find evidence. You tell your dad it's not right and he says, "Drug addicts don't have rights." What should you do?

- Warn your dad that you're going to tell your brother what is going on. Then tell him.
- If your father will punish you for this, find a more subtle way to tell your brother, such as telling him to come home when you know your dad will be in the act.
- Call a family meeting and tell your brother and your dad at the same time that you've been put in an unfair situation and you'd like them to resolve it.

3 Essay Embarrassment

Your best friend Raymond isn't in class today. Your English teacher loved his last essay so much, he wants to read it aloud to the class. But you know how private Raymond is about his writing. What should you do?

- Ask to speak to the teacher in private. Tell him that Raymond would be very hurt by him sharing his writing with the whole class.
- Suggest aloud that you would not want your essay read in your absence, so maybe it wouldn't be right.
- If you cannot stop it from being read, tell Raymond right away.

4 LOCKER LOOKOUT

Your best friend Sally and her boyfriend Jose have just had a huge fight. He has her locker combination, and you catch him going in there, probably to plant a mean note or even wreck her stuff. What should you do?

- Confront him and ask him to stop.
- Take a friend or two with you to talk to Jose, as witnesses and as protection in case he's in a really bad mood.
- Find Sally and tell her.
- If the situation seems serious, report it to a trustworthy teacher.

5 Mail Carrier

You and your friend find a letter on the sidewalk. It's addressed to someone down the street. But your friend is so curious, she decides to open it. What should you do?

- Explain that mail is private property and shouldn't be opened.
- If the mail is read, inform the owner of the letter that the letter has been opened and read.
- If you tell the owner of the letter what has happened, it's up to you to name names or not.

Continues ...

⑥ FAMILY SECRET

Ravi has a secret, something about his family, that he's not supposed to tell. You watch as your friends try to pry it out of him. You can see he's breaking down and may give in. What should you do?

- Tell Ravi in front of everyone that you respect his privacy.
- Change the topic of conversation to suggest you all go somewhere to get everyone's mind off Ravi and his private information.

⑧ Medical Intelligence

Your friend's father has just been diagnosed with prostate cancer. He's very embarrassed and doesn't want anyone to know. Your friend says it's okay for you to tell your parents, which you do. Then you hear your mother telling a neighbour over the phone a few days later. What should you do?

⑦ Kiss and Tell

Everyone knows who Kathryn kissed last Saturday night. The giggles are following her everywhere. But she has no idea her secret has been told. What should you do?

- Tell Kathryn in private that her story has been told.
- Refuse to spread the gossip any further.

- Ask your mom to not tell anyone else.
- Ask her to try to contain the secret by asking her friends to not tell others.
- Warn your friend that the secret is out.

DID YOU KNOW?

- The definition of privacy is changing, mainly because of technology.

Laws may soon be changed to deal with: the rights of an

9 ⑨ LOVE SONG

Your friend Jake has written a beautiful song for a girl he's got a secret crush on. There's always a guitar around when you hang out with your group of pals, so everyone has heard it a million times. One night at a party, another friend from the gang starts playing the song, and the girl is at the party! What should you do?

- Without letting everyone know why or what the song is about, get your friend to stop singing.
- Tell Jake that the song might have been played. You may or may not want to say who sang it.

10 ⑩ A LEAK IN CYBERSPACE

A few of you are playing around on the computer one night, and you decide to play a joke on a friend. You're going to sign him up on a porn Web site. Before you realize what's happened, someone has entered your friend's address, phone number, and e-mail onto the Web site. What should you do?

- Get your friends to stop what they're doing right away. It's no longer just a fun prank: they've leaked personal information to an unsafe source.
- Contact your friend right away and tell him what's happened. Suggest he doesn't open any unfamiliar e-mails.

employer to control what an employee does on his or her computer;

Internet service providers giving up names of customers

to the police; what Web sites can do with private information;

where it is acceptable to videotape people.

More Help

It takes time and practice to learn the skills in this book. There are many ways to deal with privacy issues, but only you know what feels right for you in different situations. In the end, the best response is the one that prevents everyone from being hurt or treated unfairly.

If you need more information or someone to talk to, these resources might help.

Helplines

Kids Help Phone (Canada) 1-800-668-6868
Youth Crisis Hotline (USA) 1-800-448-4663

Web sites

Canadian Safe School Network: www.cssn.org
Kids Help Phone: www.kidshelp.sympatico.ca
Be Web Aware: www.bewebaware.ca
Privacy Commission of Canada: www.privcom.gc.ca

Books

Alma by William Bell. Doubleday Canada, 2003.
Boy O'Boy by Brian Doyle. Groundwood Books, 2003.
The Breadwinner by Deborah Ellis. Groundwood Books, 2001.
Chandra's Secrets by Allan Stratton. Annick Press, 2004.
Jake, Reinvented by Gordon Korman. Scholastic Canada, 2003.
Making the Grade by H.G. Sotzek. Vanwell Publishing, 2003.
Ready to Run by Beverly Scudamore. James Lorimer & Co., 2006.
What They Don't Know by Anita Horrocks. Fitzhenry & Whiteside, 1999.

Other titles in the Deal With It series:

Arguing: Deal with it word by word by Elaine Slavens, illustrated by Steven Murray.
Authority: Deal with it before it deals with you by Anne Marie Aikins, illustrated by Steven Murray.
Bullying: Deal with it before push comes to shove by Elaine Slavens, illustrated by Brooke Kerrigan.
Competition: Deal with it from start to finish by Mireille Messier, illustrated by Steven Murray.
Fighting: Deal with it without coming to blows by Elaine Slavens, illustrated by Steven Murray.
Girlness: Deal with it body and soul by Diane Peters, illustrated by Steven Murray.
Gossip: Deal with it before word gets around by Catherine Rondina, illustrated by Dan Workman.
Guyness: Deal with it body and soul by Steve Pitt, illustrated by Steven Murray.
Lying: Deal with it straight up by Catherine Rondina, illustrated by Dan Workman.
Misconduct: Deal with it without bending the rules by Anne Marie Aikins, illustrated by Steven Murray.
Peer Pressure: Deal with it without losing your cool by Elaine Slavens, illustrated by Ben Shannon.
Racism: Deal with it before it gets under your skin by Anne Marie Aikins, illustrated by Steven Murray.
Rudeness: Deal with it if you please by Catherine Rondina, illustrated by Dan Workman.

Text copyright © 2006 by Diane Peters
Illustrations copyright © 2006 by Jeremy Tankard

James Lorimer & Company Ltd. acknowledges the support of the Ontario Arts Council. We acknowledge the support of the Government of Canada through the Book Publishing Industry Development Program (BPIDP) for our publishing activities. We acknowledge the support of the Canada Council for the Arts for our publishing program. We acknowledge the support of the Government of Ontario through the Ontario Media Development Corporation's Ontario Book Initiative.

The Canada Council | Le Conseil des Arts
for the Arts | du Canada

ONTARIO ARTS COUNCIL
CONSEIL DES ARTS DE L'ONTARIO

Design: Blair Kerrigan/Glyphics

Library and Archives Canada Cataloguing in Publication

Peters, Diane

Privacy : deal with it like nobody's business / by Diane Peters ; illustrated by Jeremy Tankard.

Includes bibliographical references.
ISBN 10: 1-55028-907-1
ISBN 13: 978-1-55028-907-7

1. Privacy--Juvenile literature. 2. Trust--Juvenile literature.
I. Tankard, Jeremy II. Title.

BF637.P74P48 2006   j177   C2006-900200-2

James Lorimer & Company Ltd., Publishers
317 Adelaide Street West, Suite #1002
Toronto, Ontario
M5V 1P9
www.lorimer.ca

Distributed in the United States by:
Orca Book Publishers
P.O. Box 468, Custer, WA
USA 98240-0468

Printed and bound in China